101 Questions and Answers on Catholic Marriage Preparation

101 QUESTIONS AND ANSWERS ON CATHOLIC MARRIAGE PREPARATION

Rebecca Nappi
Daniel Kendall, SJ

PAULIST PRESS
New York/Mahwah, N.J.

Cover design by Cynthia Dunne
Book design by Theresa M. Sparacio

Library of Congress Cataloging-in-Publication Data

Nappi, Rebecca.
    101 questions and answers on Catholic marriage preparation / Rebecca Nappi, Daniel Kendall.
        p.   cm.
    Includes bibliographical references.
    ISBN 0-8091-4291-0 (alk. paper)
    1. Marriage—Religious aspects—Catholic Church—Miscellanea. 2. Marriage service—Miscellanea. I. Title: One hundred one questions and answers on Catholic marriage preparation. II. Title: One hundred and one questions and answers on Catholic marriage preparation. III. Kendall, Daniel. IV. Title.

BX2250.N3 2005
261.8′3581—dc22

                                                                    2004015171

Published by Paulist Press
997 Macarthur Boulevard
Mahwah, New Jersey 07430

www.paulistpress.com

Printed and bound in the
United States of America

CONTENTS

Contents   xiii

To Tony Wadden,
friend, husband, and constant
source of encouragement

ACKNOWLEDGMENTS

In any project that takes place over a long period of time, such as the writing of a book, countless people give suggestions on one or more aspects of the work. Though a danger is always present that someone will be inadvertently overlooked, we would like to thank those who helped us, especially Christopher Bellitto, the Academic Editor of Paulist Press, for his encouragement and patience. Father Gerald O'Collins, SJ, provided us with initial ideas and checked the text for style and errors. Others to whom we are grateful include Bill and Kathy Bezy, Shannon McMillen Evans, and Father Jeffrey LaBelle, SJ. We'd also like to thank the four couples from St. Thomas More Parish in Spokane, Washington, who have supported one another for years in a Marriage Encounter Love Circle: Grant and Julie Becherini, Steve and Sherry Gonnella, Rosalie and Jack Nourse, and Al and Sharon Pry. And finally, a thank-you to Father Dan's parents, Bob and Loretto Kendall, and Becky's parents, Laura and Joe Nappi. Their enduring marriages provided us with a framework from which to grow, work, and love in the world.

PREFACE

On May 17, 1985, Becky Nappi married Tony Wadden at the Jesuit House Chapel on the campus of Gonzaga University in Spokane, Washington. Father Dan Kendall, a Jesuit priest who teaches theology at San Francisco University, presided at the wedding.

Each summer, Father Dan visited Tony and Becky in Spokane. One summer Becky, a journalist at *The Spokesman-Review* in Spokane, suggested that the two of them collaborate on a marriage book. Father Dan had presided at many weddings over the past thirty years of his priesthood and had written several theology books. In the course of her journalism career, Becky had reported several stories on what makes marriages work. So the two of them felt these experiences would serve them well in writing together about marriage.

On the surface, Father Dan and Becky seem an unlikely "couple" to collaborate on a marriage book. Father Dan is a priest who has never married, of course. Becky married at age thirty, kept her own name, and people who don't know her well tell her she seems too independent to be married.

But this unlikely collaboration worked out well. The two — although not experts on weddings and marriage — learned from the real experts: dozens of married couples. They asked questions. They listened. They learned. Father Dan contacted many of the couples at whose weddings he had presided. Becky talked with family and friends. Both Father Dan and Becky sat down with four couples who had been married an average of thirty years each. The couples belong to a "Love Circle" at St. Thomas More Parish in Spokane, Washington. A Love Circle is a support group of married couples that forms following a Marriage Encounter weekend. The Love Circle couples have met once a month together for fifteen years. They provided great details and advice in an afternoon discussion with Father Dan and Becky.

While researching and writing this book together, Father Dan and Becky also witnessed the end of one marriage both were close to. In Becky's life, three marriages of close friends hit major snags and all three couples considered divorce. So far the couples' marriages remain intact, because all sought counseling when the problems grew serious. The end of the one marriage, and the troubles in these long-term marriages, provided Becky and Father Dan with strong examples of the issues that can start small in a marriage and grow so large over the years that they threaten the entire union.

During the course of researching and writing this book, Becky learned that couples should never grow smug about their marriages. Marriage is a sacred union—and a fragile one. Marriage requires vigilance, kindness, and constant care. It takes work to keep a marriage strong.

Father Dan appreciated the fact that having good preparation and facing issues before the wedding make for a happier marriage. Important issues do not "always work out in the end" unless they are faced, and many difficulties and hard feelings can be avoided by discussing them before the marriage ceremony.

Father Dan and Becky are grateful to all the married couples, young and old, who provided questions and answers for this book, and they hope that the book will answer many of the questions engaged and newly married couples ask. They anticipate that the book will spark conversation among engaged couples. Frank and open talk before the wedding is essential—for couples and for communities. And so, let the conversation begin.

ONE

WHAT IS CATHOLIC MARRIAGE?

Historical and Scriptural Background

1. What is the Catholic understanding of Christian marriage?

Catholics understand Christian marriage as a lifelong partnership between a baptized man and woman lived in the context of the church community. This union forms the basic community of both church and civil society. As such it affects more than just the couple. Members of society closest to the couple include their relatives, friends, associates, and organizations such as their church community, businesses, and civil government. Just as the couple contributes to the larger society, so the various elements of the larger society pledge themselves to help the couple.

2. How does the wedding reflect this understanding?

A Catholic wedding ceremony reflects these elements. The man and the woman acknowledge the beginning of their lifelong partnership by asking their families, representatives of the church community, and friends to witness their commitment. A typical wedding ceremony has parents and close relatives playing prominent roles. The couple commit themselves to each other in front of a priest or deacon, witnesses they choose, and friends who want to show their support. They sign a marriage license so that the civil government will give official recognition to their permanent union and their new role in society.

3. If we are marrying each other, why do we need a church ceremony?

Catholics realize that many people hold diverse views about the church's role in a marriage ceremony. Telephone books have advertisements for wedding chapels, and people line up in city halls to have judges and justices of the peace legalize their unions. Most of these people do not want to marry in a church. Catholics see themselves as a religious community in which Jesus Christ is the central figure. Since its earliest days, Christianity has used the metaphor of marriage to show the relationship of Christ to the church (Eph 5:10–32). Therefore Christian marriage involves Jesus and the community which he founded. The couple are part of this community. Unlike an entirely civil marriage, a Catholic marriage reminds the couple that they are joining their lives together within the context of a faith community. The values to which they pledge themselves are love, permanence, and fidelity, which are not necessarily part of a ceremony performed at city hall. Symbols which Catholics use to convey these values include the site—a church—and a religious ceremony.

4. What texts in the Old Testament do Christians cite or quote in defining marriage?

The Old Testament does not have a specific section on marriage. We need, therefore, to look at various scattered passages that relate to marriage. For instance, in Genesis we are told that men and women are created as equals (1:27–28). Human sexuality and sexual union within marriage (Gen 2:24) are part of God's good creation. Sexual union is for procreation as well as for expressing love within the oneness of marriage (cf. Prov 5:15–19). The entire *Song of Songs (The Song of Solomon)* is a love dialogue between a man and a woman. The Book of Ruth tenderly describes the marriage between an Israelite and a non-Israelite.

Adultery violates the commitment inherent in marriage (Exod 20:14). Although the biblical ideal is that of a marriage that lasts a lifetime, the Mosaic law allowed a man to divorce his wife by issuing for her a bill of divorce (Deut 24:1). Generally in the Old Testament wives took care of the home while the men worked and could be leaders in society. Exceptions to this, however, include

Deborah who was a judge (Judg 4–5). Even the ideal wife of Proverbs 31 exercised considerable creativity and initiative in far-ranging projects (Prov 31:15–16): "She rises while it is still night and provides food for her household and tasks for her servant-girls. She considers a field and buys it; with the fruit of her hands she plants a vineyard."

Although polygamy is mentioned in the earlier days of Israel, by the time of Jesus monogamy was the practice.

5. Why didn't Jesus marry? Could Jesus have been married?

Though no reason is given in the New Testament for Jesus' not marrying, theologians generally contend that Jesus wanted to give himself entirely to his mission.

Some scholars have argued that Jesus must have married since otherwise his message would not have been welcomed by his Jewish audience. No one would listen to a single man. The New Testament says nothing about what Jesus did between the ages of twelve and almost thirty. On the other hand, no hard evidence exists that he was married, only conjecture. Jesus was a person who did not fit into many categories. Tradition and biblical evidence point to the fact that he remained single and yet was accepted by a large number of people.

6. What do the Gospels tell us about marriage? Were Jesus' apostles married?

During his life Jesus affirmed his Jewish heritage, but raised the discussion from observance of the law to the ideal. For instance, Jesus emphasized God's intention that marriage be a lifetime commitment: "Therefore what God has joined together, let no one separate" (Mark 10:9). He said quite explicitly that monogamy is God's plan for humanity (Matt 19:4–5). Adultery should not even be contemplated in one's heart (Matt 5:27–28). Although Jesus did not minimize sins such as adultery, he did not condemn people so much as he tried to get them to start anew (John 4:1–42). Divorce goes against God's intention that marriage be for life, but Jesus seemed to have made a concession on this point in some cases (Matt 5:32, 19:9).

The only apostle explicitly mentioned as being married is Peter. Jesus cured his mother-in-law: "He came and took her by the hand and lifted her up. Then the fever left her, and she began to serve them" (Mark 1:31). While we can conjecture about the others, the New Testament says nothing directly about their being married or not married.

7. I have heard that Paul was negative about marriage. Is this true?

While the Gospels were all written after the death of Jesus and under the influence of the emerging church, other New Testament works, especially the letters of Paul, were written earlier than the Gospels and show us how the early church looked at marriage. To understand Paul the reader needs to put him in context. At the time he wrote his earlier letters (e.g., 1 Thess and 1 Cor) he expected the world to end soon. This is seen clearly in 1 Corinthians 7. Given that situation, Paul urges Christians to remain in the state in which they currently find themselves—married or single. The end of the world will bring its tribulations. If, however, a person wishes to marry, Paul finds no wrong in that. In such a context it is difficult to assert that Paul was "against marriage."

We know that Jesus emphasized God's intention that marriage be a lifetime commitment (Mark 10:5–9; Matt 19:4–9). Pauline teaching spells this out. Ephesians emphasizes the importance of self-giving love in marriage (5:28). Sexual relations should express the oneness of marriage (1 Cor 6:12–20). Persistent immorality is unacceptable behavior for Christians (1 Cor 5:1–13; 6:12–20). Christians are urged to marry other Christians (1 Cor 7:39); through marriage a person can sanctify one's partner (1 Cor 7:12–16): "For the unbelieving husband is made holy through his wife, and the unbelieving wife is made holy through her husband." Paul allowed divorce if a marriage between a believer and nonbeliever resulted in discord. Neither Jesus nor Paul presented marriage or singleness as a second-class or less holy state than the other. In a strong statement in Galatians, Paul speaks of the equality of men and women when he says that for a Christian there is "no longer Jew or Greek, there is no longer slave or free, there is no longer male and female, for all of you are one in Christ Jesus" (3:28).

8. Today people speak about equality in marriage. Isn't Paul's—and the New Testament's—view rather one-sided and always favoring the male's role?

As much as we would like to deny any fault in Paul, the evidence is overwhelming that he often accepted the standard of first-century society as his norm in everyday affairs. The same holds true for other New Testament writers. One example of this is the prohibition about women addressing an assembly: "If there is anything they desire to know, let them ask their husbands at home" (1 Cor 14:34–35). Other examples are that wives are to be subject to their husbands (Eph 5:22) and accept their authority, and they are not outwardly to adorn themselves (1 Pet 3:1–2). These sociological statements need to be balanced by Paul's statement about the equality of all (Gal 3:28). Christianity today is not tied to first-century sociological norms. This is dramatically seen when views about slavery in scripture—"Slaves, obey your earthly masters with fear and trembling…" (Eph 6:5)—are contrasted with current views about the intrinsic evil of slavery.

Church Teachings

9. How has the Catholic concept of marriage evolved? Have Catholics always looked at marriage the same way as they do now?

Within the Catholic Church the definition of marriage has varied over time. For instance, a typical Catholic view before Vatican II (1962–65) was that of "a sacrament in which two marriageable people of different sexes associate in an undivided life-communion by mutual agreement for the generation and education of offspring, and in which they receive grace for the fulfillment of the special duties of their state." The primary purpose of marriage was the "generation and bringing-up of children. The secondary purpose [was] the mutual help and the morally regulated satisfaction of the sex urge."[1] In contrast Vatican II (1962–65) did not make this distinction between the primary and secondary purposes but called marriage a lifetime intimate partnership of life and love.[2]

10. What changes in the Catholic view of marriage did Vatican II bring about?

The first definition in the previous answer is more "act centered," while the second is "contextualized." A popular way of characterizing the difference between these two definitions is to say that the first resembles a contract while the second is a covenant. A contract looks at whether a person has fulfilled certain legal stipulations (things), whereas a covenant looks at personal commitment (people). It's a more holistic approach. Covenant also has biblical roots which highlight relationships. In the past the church emphasized making sure the marriage was valid and the knot was securely tied. Today the church focuses on marriage preparation to make certain that it will be a happy journey together. This also accords with the twentieth- and twenty-first century emphasis on personalism in which people and their relationships are the center of theory and practice as opposed to a rigorous application of a philosophical or theological theory which does not consider the context.

11. Has the official church subsequently offered further teaching on marriage?

Most of the church's comments in recent years have built on Vatican II's approach. For instance, Pope John Paul II reaffirmed Vatican II's teaching in an apostolic exhortation *(Familiaris Corsortio*—a 1981 document on the family in the modern era). Negatively, the Vatican has spoken about abuses of marriage in documents such as *The Truth and Meaning of Human Sexuality* (issued in 1995 concerning sex education), *Preparation for the Sacrament of Marriage* (which gave much attention in 1996 to the dangers the partners and the family face), and *Family, Marriage, and "De Facto" Unions* (a warning in 2000 about the bad effects which "living together" have on marriage in general).

12. Why do Catholics make a big deal about marriage being a *sacrament*, while other Christians usually say nothing about this?

A sacrament is an encounter with God in a church community setting. When Catholics speak of sacraments they usually mean one of seven formal ritual actions that have come to be called the *seven sacraments.* Many Protestants recognize only two sacraments—baptism and the Lord's Supper. Yet they also have ceremonies for the other five ritual actions which Catholics call *sacraments.* For Catholics to speak of *sacramental* marriage means that God, the worshiping Christian community, and the couple themselves are involved in their lives together. Catholics recognize the marriage between two Protestants as *sacramental,* even though the two persons themselves might not think in those categories since they do not recognize seven sacraments.

13. Is there a difference between the way Catholics and Protestants look at marriage?

Not really. In general Protestants also define marriage in terms of covenant. Although this might differ in individual groups, mainline faith confessions such as Lutherans and Episcopalians speak of covenant rather than contract. Even the ceremonies are similar. They all consist of scripture readings, exchange of consent, and (usually) the giving of rings. The consent speaks of the permanence of the union and the fidelity of the partners to each other.

14. What is the difference between a *sacramental* and a *nonsacramental* marriage?

While we do not know how God acts in individual cases, in popular conversation a nonsacramental marriage is one in which God and the worshiping Christian community are not part of the marriage. For instance, a marriage between two unbaptized persons is not a sacramental marriage.

Theologian Jean Corbon described the difference this way: "What the sacrament adds is not so much the blessing of the couple (every marriage, after all, is holy) as the love of Christ and his Church in which the husband and wife will share."[3]

15. Has the church's view on "mixed" marriages changed in recent years?

To state that the Catholic Church was against marriages between Catholics and non-Catholics is to make a profound understatement. Before 1940, in many U.S. dioceses, such a wedding was not allowed in a church, so it took place at home.

For example, Father Dan's mother and her sister got engaged on the same day in 1936. Father Dan's mother married his father, a Catholic, in the parish church. The sister who was engaged to a non-Catholic was not allowed to get married in the parish church, so the ceremony took place in her parents' living room.

Four years later, more concessions were made to non-Catholics. In 1940, a third sister was allowed to marry in the church even though she married a Presbyterian. However, "mixed" marriage couples of that time were not allowed to stand, or kneel, beyond the communion rail in the sanctuary. No Mass was allowed nor could the nuptial blessing be given. They needed to promise in writing that their children would be raised as Catholics. Austerity and lack of publicity marked the almost-shameful occasion.

It's important to remember that the secular culture of the time was also strict when it came to weddings. For instance, in a 1952 etiquette book written by Amy Vanderbilt, she made it clear that a woman's maid of honor should not be a divorcee or a woman who is "very much older than the bride."[4]

Today, the church and the rest of the culture have relaxed these rules of exclusion. Today, when a Catholic marries a non-Catholic, Mass is allowed for these weddings, as well as the nuptial blessing. The liturgy is flexible, with the couple picking the readings and the format of the ceremony—and even writing their own vows. Sometimes one of the spouses has even been married before in the church, and that marriage has been annulled.

16. Do we, my non-Catholic intended spouse and I, need to make special promises such as raising our children as Catholics?

Today the church asks the Catholic party to promise in writing that future children will be raised as Catholics. The non-Catholic is asked to agree to raise children as Catholics but is not required to sign an agreement. Refusal to make this promise will usually rule out a Catholic wedding.

17. Is marriage a lower state than religious life?

When a person asks a question about something being "higher" or "lower," that person must have some type of norm in mind. Sometimes people will take 1 Corinthians 7:38 out of context to assert that marriage is a lower state than religious life. They believe that ideally a religious person can be totally dedicated to God while a married person is distracted by a spouse and family. Ultimately all of us will be judged on what we have done for God and our neighbor, not whether we did it as a member of a religious order or as someone married. All Christians are called to lives that are holy and worthy of their deep union with Christ through baptism. What could be higher than totally dedicating ourselves to the ministries to which God has called us?

18. Why can't priests marry?

Because of various problems with inheritance and church property, the Western part of the church has demanded celibacy of its clergy for many hundreds of years. That practice does not apply to Catholic churches in the Eastern part of the world. There we find a married clergy. Obviously people frequently ask these days whether the circumstances which caused the Western practice of celibacy to begin should still be the norm. Some say celibacy today is intended to free up a priest for greater service to the community, while others believe it is more of a historical and economic construct.

19. I don't care about where I get married. My family is putting pressure on me to marry in the Catholic Church. What should I do?

As mentioned in the answers to questions 10 and 12, a Catholic marriage involves God, the community, and the couple themselves. If you do not wish God or the Christian community to be part of your marriage, then why go through a Catholic ceremony?

It would be somewhat hypocritical to stand in front of a community and pledge your love and commitment if you do not believe in that community or want that community's support. On the other hand, other considerations play a large part in desiring a church wedding, such as family, friends, and the spouses' relatives. This is something you need to discuss with a priest or deacon to come up with the best solution.

And sometimes other family members recognize the deeper meaning of marrying in the church, something you might not be able to appreciate fully at this time in your life. When Becky married Tony she was thirty years old and, like many baby-boomer Catholics, she had quit attending church throughout her twenties. Her parents, as well as Tony and Father Dan, all encouraged a Catholic wedding and Becky went along with it, but said at the time it didn't matter to her where she married. In fact, she had a plan to be married by a judge in a ceremony in her parents' back yard. Becky and Tony married in the church, with Father Dan presiding. When Becky was in her thirties and forties, her spiritual journey led her back to a Catholic parish and faith community. She often thanks those in her life who understood the importance of a Catholic wedding. She feels they "kept the faith" for her until she was ready to journey there again herself. If she had married Tony in the back yard eighteen years ago, she would have wanted a church ceremony at this point in her life. In addition to the spiritual benefits, those people who kept the faith for her spared her the expense of a second wedding in the church!

TWO

WHAT IS MARRIAGE PREPARATION?

General Planning

20. Why are we required to do marriage preparation?

Marriage is probably the most important decision most people will make in their lives. Yet people often spend more time and energy preparing for college, career, and choosing a place to live. Even learning how to drive a car requires a semester's worth of lessons and several tests. Shouldn't marriage, this most important life step, deserve even more time and energy?

21. When and why did the church institute the six-months "waiting" period between making the initial arrangements and the actual wedding ceremony?

The long waiting period is something that is unique to the United States. It was instituted in the early 1980s by the Bishops' Conference because of the skyrocketing divorce rate. It also came at a time when church annulments became easier to obtain, and the awareness of the frequency of divorce became very apparent to church leaders. Now couples who wish to marry in the Catholic Church are required to declare their intent six months before the proposed wedding, during which time they need to complete all the preparations. In some parts of the country people plan the reception, the limos, the flowers, over a *year* in advance. That gives perspective to how carefully the couple should plan their life together.

22. Since the church asks us to wait six months before we marry, what are the preparations we are expected to complete in the meantime?

Although six months seems to be a long time, most couples are surprised at how quickly the time passes. During that time the couple needs to do all the church and civil paperwork for the wedding. They also need to make an *Engaged Encounter* (or go through some other program of preparation, such as the *Pre-Cana* Conference, that their diocese provides), and take a communication assessment such as the FOCCUS. For more about FOCCUS, see our answer to question 33.

23. My doctor recently told me that I am pregnant. Should my future spouse and I ask for an exception to the six-months preparation policy?

This question is not easy to answer. Various factors need to be considered such as: How long have you known each other? Do both of you really want to marry, or is one of you being forced into it? And so on. By itself pregnancy is not considered a good reason to ask for an exception to diocesan policy. People in a state of panic are usually not in a good position to make reasonable decisions. Talking this over with the priest or deacon or counselor is the first step before asking for an exemption to the diocesan policy. In our culture being pregnant without marriage does not carry the stigma it once did. It's no longer as shocking or as shameful. This understanding makes it easier for couples to really think out the best course of action for themselves and their child.

24. Is *Engaged Encounter* mandatory for all people who want to marry in the church?

The *Engaged Encounter* is a weekend experience in which several couples meet with older and younger married couples. The "team" presents their experience on a variety of issues— money, sex, decision-making, and the like—and then invites the engaged couples to write their reactions in notebooks and dialogue about it. The format is standard throughout the United States, although it is updated on a regular basis. The *Engaged Encounter* is frequently done in more than one language for people who will feel more at home in their own language. In most dioceses in the United States it is mandatory unless it is impossible for the couple to make the Encounter. Instead of the *Engaged Encounter,* some dioceses ask the couple to attend one or two sessions of a *Pre-Cana Conference,* or something similar. In any case each diocese usually provides alternatives if a couple cannot attend the standard preparation.

25. I have some personal difficulties with the people who run the *Engaged Encounter* in the area where I live. Do I have options other than the *Engaged Encounter*?

The church is trying to get away from the "one size fits all" mentality. Yes, if you have difficulties like you just mentioned, the *Engaged Encounter* is probably not for you. Most dioceses have alternative programs such as those where you meet with married couples on an individual basis. The *Engaged Encounter* has the advantage that couples are not alone; other couples are with you, and you can profit from their experience just as you can from the team presentations.

26. Is a celibate priest in any position to talk about marriage to engaged people?

Obviously the best people to talk to engaged couples are people who are happily married. These days the preparations for marriage are given by lay people. A priest, especially one who has handled many annulment cases, is in a position to tell people some of the pitfalls which have caused divorce. In an analogy, a doctor does not always need to have suffered the illness of the patient in order to give good advice about what to avoid.

When Father Dan is asked to do marriage preparation with a couple, he directs them to resources that are available, such as *Engaged Encounter,* foccus, *Cana Conferences,* and so on. He sees his role as making the couple comfortable in their preparation and facilitating the ceremony. Frequently the perspective of a third party (such as a priest or married couple) can better help a couple in areas such as finance even though that third party will not be directly involved in making decisions.

27. My intended spouse and I have been living together for almost two years. Now we are ready to marry, so we don't think we need a marriage preparation course. Won't the preparation of having already lived together greatly help our marriage succeed?

Though living together is a common practice now in our culture among Catholics and non-Catholics, this practice can actually work against the success of the marriage. In more than half of all first marriages, couples lived together first, according to a 2002 report by the *National Marriage Project* at Rutgers University in New Jersey.[5] Couples believe that "trying it out" first will help them understand each other better before making that serious commitment of marriage. But many studies have shown that couples who live together before marrying have a higher risk of divorce, perhaps fifty percent higher, than couples who do not live together. And the longer the couples cohabit before marriage, the greater the risk of divorce. What's going on? Researchers aren't sure, but they have theories. Perhaps couples who lived together first feel less commitment in general toward the relationship, and when the rough times come along, it's easier to split rather than do the hard work to deepen the commitment. Or perhaps the couples who live together first had doubts about the relationship from the beginning and when the marriage begins to falter, the trouble confirms those early doubts. Ultimately, marriage is a leap of faith. Many long-time married couples will tell you that they knew very quickly, sometimes even after a few dates, that their spouse was "the one" they wished to spend the rest of their lives with. And the commitment to marriage seemed the only way to solidify that feeling of rightness. So they made the leap. Living together before marriage is like making a half-leap. It doesn't necessarily doom a marriage, but it might make it harder to sustain.

28. Those banns that are posted with people's names—what are they all about?

Before Vatican II people needed to present themselves to the priest only four or five weeks before their wedding. The "banns" were published on the three Sundays before the wedding as a way to ask the community if anyone was aware of any impediments to the wedding. Now, with the six-month marriage preparation requirement and the need to plan weddings well in advance, word about weddings is usually known for more than three weeks before the ceremony, but the procedure is still frequently followed.

29. My intended spouse and I both work and live in cities distant from each other. How can we go through a marriage preparation program together?

If you are engaged you no doubt will be seeing one another during a six-month period. When you allocate your time, you need to set a value to preparing well for what is probably the most important decision you will ever make. If you have a situation where you cannot make an *Engaged Encounter* or *Pre-Cana Conference,* you need to talk with the priest or deacon who is preparing the wedding. There are usually other options available. This might entail going though preparation in another diocese.

30. My intended spouse was married before but obtained a church annulment. Do we still need to go through marriage preparation?

The answer is yes. Most people in this situation want a full marriage preparation. Not only will you know your future spouse better as a result, but also both of you might be able to avoid the pitfalls which caused the first marriage to end. Remember: you will be entering a new relationship. You want it to be a happy sacramental union, so it is well worth good preparation.

31. My fiancée is non-Catholic. Do we still have to go through Catholic marriage preparation?

The answer again is yes. In fact since the two of you do not share a common faith community, it is perhaps more important to talk out how you will face future issues in this regard. Most non-Catholic churches also include this aspect in their marriage preparation programs.

32. How does marriage preparation, especially sharing experiences with other couples, help the chances of having a successful marriage?

When you plan a trip, you consult travel books and magazines, and you talk with other people who have already traveled to your destination. They recount their experiences, recommend hotels and restaurants, and warn you away from negative aspects such as tourist traps. Even after all the planning and advice from others, your trip will be uniquely yours.

Marriage preparation, and conversations with long-time married couples, is like trip planning. It will give you a head start on your marriage journey, especially when it comes to pitfalls to avoid. Long-time married couples will help you most by talking about the reality of marriage.

For instance, Becky's sister Janice had been married fourteen years when Becky was preparing for her wedding. Janice took Becky aside one day and said, "Don't expect your husband to be all your fun. Be sure to remember to have fun with your girlfriends and your sisters." The underlying message was this: the other partner in your marriage should not be expected to fulfill all your social needs. If you don't expect this, you won't feel disappointed when it doesn't happen. It's the best marriage advice Becky received and she now passes it along to all engaged couples she talks with.

33. I have heard that people are required to undergo a written test to see if they are compatible with each other. What is this "test" all about? If we fail it can we still marry in the church? What areas does it cover?

There are several "tests" which various dioceses use. The most common is called FOCCUS. It is not so much a test as a questionnaire inventory on the areas of finances, sexuality, children, in-laws, and communication. The couple separately answer the same questions. The responses are then compared and graphed, and the couple will discover those areas in which they think the same way, and in which they differ. This gives them an opportunity to discuss these areas and find out why in some areas their views are divergent. There is no pass or fail for such an inventory. Even when the results show that a couple are not compatible in several areas, that in itself does not necessarily delay a wedding.

Finances

34. Why do finances always seem to be the first question people want to discuss?

Most couples will admit that many of their fights revolve around money, especially in the first year of marriage, and then again when a couple's economic situation changes—for better or for worse. Money is loaded with symbolism. Each partner was raised in a family where money was valued, handled, and regarded in specific ways. And rarely is their understanding of money, as experienced in childhood, similar. Often partners were raised in families of differing socio-economic status.

Marriage preparation is the best time to confront money issues in depth. Couples should ask each other very specific questions. How much debt do you have going into the marriage? How much debt feels comfortable? Are you the type who pays off credit cards every month? Or the type who doesn't mind paying finance charges to be able to buy things now? Will you merge both of your earnings into a general fund or keep separate accounts? How much of your income will go to savings, charity, your church community? These might seem like trivial details, but discussing them in depth will get at core values that you bring into your marriage.

One couple Becky knows has fought for forty years over the same money issue. The husband pays off his credit cards each month and is the last person to reach for his wallet to pay for dinners out. His wife has thousands of dollars in credit card debt and possesses a card or two her husband doesn't know about. When out to dinner with others, she is the first to reach for the bill. She calls him cheap. He thinks she's an irresponsible spendthrift. The deeper issue for him is his emotional tightness. And she seeks recognition through buying gifts and paying for others.

Bottom line? Talk about money during marriage preparation. And if money disagreements continue to surface in your discussions, pay attention!

Sexuality

35. What aspects of sexuality present challenges?

For a culture that is seemingly so open about sex, we are poorly educated about, and even poorer at communicating about, the reality of sexuality within marriage. Our parents don't talk to us about it, and sex education in schools is narrowly focused. The topic is rarely discussed even among close friends. Sex is still considered a private matter between husband and wife and for the most part, it should be. The problem is that couples often lack the skills and the confidence to discuss sex with one another, because there is so little guidance available.

Couples in marriage preparation should discuss honestly their feelings about sex, and how sexual activity was discussed or viewed in their families of origin. If it was seen as something shameful, your future husband or wife might bring that attitude to the marriage bed. Women and men who have been sexually abused as children can also have some problems with sexual intimacy. There are many good books available about marriage sexuality. Reading those books together might be the most comfortable way to educate yourselves about sex within a marriage and communicate about it, too.

Sex is one of the best expressions of the sacred union between husband and wife, but poor education and lack of communication about it can take away from the sacredness of sex. That's why it's important to practice communicating about sex early in your relationship.

36. How realistic is the sex you see between couples in movies versus the reality of sex within marriage?

Even movie stars admit that the lovemaking scenes they participate in on the screen have no basis in reality. Lovemaking on tabletops, for instance, is almost a physical impossibility! Movie sex also conveys the idea that sex is *the* most important part of a relationship when, in reality, it is just one part of a continuum of intimacy. And the movies usually depict sex between couples who are new to each other and not the mature lovemaking that happens between long-married couples.

Also, few people in the real world have those movie star bodies. Movies are supposed to be fantasies, but the danger is that couples use the fiction world of film to measure their own sexual relationship, and they then feel inadequate.

Children

37. My future spouse and I do not want children. There are enough people in the world and we do not wish to add to the population explosion. Why does the church frown on this attitude?

Since marriage is supposed to be an intimate partnership of life and love, it seems contradictory to exclude the fruit of such a partnership. Sometimes such a relationship is called "married singles," where the partners want to share nothing. By its very nature marriage should be life-giving, open, and a witness to the couple's life and love. In this regard the couple should reflect the love and life-giving God in whose image they were created (Gen 1:27).

38. How can we decide together how many children to have and when to have them?

Older couples with grown children will often tell you that there was never a "right" time to have children, but somehow things worked out okay when their children came along. There's no perfect time in a couple's relationship to start a family. Younger couples often lack money and time, but they have energy to chase little ones around. Older couples who have postponed starting a family to settle into careers sometimes run into fertility problems. Or, when they do have children, they have plenty of money and resources, but they're exhausted! The discussions about when to have the first child should begin during marriage preparation.

You can discuss how many children you would like, but sometimes God and nature have other plans. There's still a lot of mystery to the timing and number of children, and being open to that mystery can be both a relief and a grace for a couple.

If either partner has children from a previous marriage or relationship, it's essential to discuss during marriage preparation the ways in which those children will be incorporated into your marriage. Disagreements about stepchildren can torpedo a marriage within the first few years. If you keep your focus on the best situation for the children, it will help. And counseling might be needed to sort out all the emotions and demands stepchildren add to a new marriage.

39. Is it true that artificial birth control is condemned by the church?

Though the official church position against artificial contraception is clear, Catholic hierarchies in various countries have interpreted this teaching in various ways. After Pope Paul VI issued a famous encyclical on the subject, *Humanae Vitae* (1968), at least ten national hierarchies (Austria, Belgium, Canada, East Germany, France, Indonesia, The Netherlands, Scandinavia, Switzerland, West Germany), supported by prominent theologians (for instance Karl Rahner and Bernard Häring), advised people that other probable opinions on the subject existed. These hierarchies urged people to consider their own life situations when responding to papal teaching. The issue of birth control remains a tense one in the Catholic faith tradition. In a 1980 meeting on the family in Rome, Archbishop John Quinn of San Francisco cited studies that showed "nearly 80 percent of U.S. Catholic married women use contraceptives" and "only 29 percent of U.S. Catholic priests consider artificial contraception intrinsically wrong."[6] During marriage preparation, couples should discuss this issue with the priest who will preside at their wedding and with married Catholic couples who have grappled with the dilemma in their own marriages.

40. How is natural family planning different from the rhythm method my grandparents practiced?

If couples choose the Natural Family Planning method, known as NFP, they should know that it differs a great deal from the so-called rhythm method practiced in their grandparents' generation. The rhythm method was based on flawed knowledge of women's menstrual cycles and taught women that they were infertile several days a month. This general advice did not take into consideration that a woman's ovulation pattern fluctuates and is unique to each woman. That's why Catholic families of older generations grew so large.

The Natural Family Planning method relies on signals from each woman's body, such as temperature fluctuations, to let her know fertile and infertile days. How effective is NFP? Proponents claim as high as 99 percent, but other studies show between 60 and 80 percent effective. Catholics are not the only experts on NFP. Other faith traditions and people into holistic health care also teach and write about it. If interested, simply type "Natural Family Planning" into any Internet search engine. You'll find thousands of sources to investigate, and almost all dioceses offer NFP classes.

41. The inability to have children receives much scrutiny today. What changes in attitude occur if a couple discovers they cannot have children?

Infertility, which is on the rise in our culture, can become an issue in a marriage. Engaged couples should discuss how they would feel if they faced infertility. They should also discuss their attitudes toward adoption.

Couples grappling with infertility find that others often tread on their personal lives. They can feel a lot of pressure from family and friends to try every available treatment, no matter the expense. Or others will advise them to just "relax" or plan an adoption. Becky found out three years into her marriage that she was infertile. Even though she talks, and writes, very openly about many topics, she was surprised how personal the infertility issue felt to her. It was a private matter between Becky and Tony, as it is for most couples.

Hopefully, infertility will not become an issue; it tests marriages to the core. But if it does, and you've discussed it before marriage, it will help with decisions along the way. One couple, friends of Becky and Tony, knew before marrying that fertility might be an issue, because the woman had been exposed to DES while in the womb. DES, a synthetic hormone, was given to mothers years ago in the mistaken belief it prevented miscarriages. Instead, it damaged the reproductive systems of the babies the mothers carried. Becky's friend was up front with her fiancé about the DES before they were married. The couple did experience fertility challenges, and ultimately adopted, and it was still very difficult. But because they had talked about it while engaged, it made it much easier to face the challenges together.

In-Laws

42. In-laws are another of the big areas for discussion. What issues do they present?

Faith Spotted Eagle, a Dakota Indian, is a friend of Becky's. She once told her that in older times in her native culture, a mother-in-law could never address a son-in-law directly. They always had to speak through a third person. Faith's tribe knew, long before comedians told mother-in-law jokes, that the in-law relationship was complex and potentially explosive for a marriage. Each person in the couple comes from a family with its unique values, rituals, habits, beliefs, and quirks. Often families believe their ways are the best ways.

In marriage preparation, it's important to talk honestly about how much time each partner expects to spend with his or her own family and with the in-laws. If you will be living in the same town as one set of parents, it's important to balance time with the set of parents who live out of town. One couple Tony and Becky know well married young almost thirty years ago. The wife's family lived a thousand miles away; the husband's family lived ninety miles away. In the first nine weeks of their marriage, the husband's parents came to town and spent seven of those nine first weekends with the young couple who gave up their bed for the parents. The young bride didn't like it at all, but didn't know if this was a "normal" in-law practice to expect. It wasn't.

It's essential as a couple to set limits and boundaries and to establish your own traditions. These habits should start in marriage preparation. Remember that as you join together in marriage, you create your own family unit, separate from the families you grew up in. Creating a new family unit, starting with just the two of you, should be a couple's top priority. The sooner in your relationship you establish that "the one who made them at the beginning made them male and female," the easier it will be to leave "father and mother...and become one flesh" (Matt 19:4–5).

43. Am I supposed to love my in-laws right away? Should I call them "Mom" and "Dad"?

We sometimes wrongly assume that daughters- and sons-in-law should automatically bond with each other's parents. But in reality relationships between in-laws evolve like all other friendships. The relationships take time and energy. Some people will click right away. Others will never see eye-to-eye.

To establish what to call your in-laws, ask directly: "What shall I call you?" If they say they will leave it up to you, then be honest about what names sound and feel comfortable to you. If you start out the marriage calling your in-laws by their first names, and then as you get to know them better and wish to call them Mom and Dad, then you can make the switch—with their permission, of course. The important thing to keep in mind is this: love of in-laws does not happen automatically just because you've married into the family. If it does, great. But most often it takes time and effort. Be patient.

44. My future father-in-law is very sarcastic and uses teasing as a way to show affection. It makes me uncomfortable. I've asked my fiancé to confront him about it, but so far he hasn't. Am I being too sensitive?

You have a right to your feelings. Your only mistake here is to expect your fiancé to confront his father. It is your responsibility to talk to your future father-in-law directly and point out how his communication style makes you uncomfortable. You expect your fiancé to do your hard communication work, when it is really your responsibility. By not doing it yourself, you are putting your husband in the middle and in an unspoken way asking him to "choose" between you and his father.

Direct communication, in a non-accusing way, is always the best form of in-law communication. It's hard and sometimes awkward, but it will pay off as the marriage matures. The sooner you establish this pattern, the better.

Becky is from a big Italian family that gets together quite a lot. When Becky and Tony first married, Tony made it clear that he wouldn't attend all the Nappi family functions. When Becky arrived alone, family members quizzed her about Tony's whereabouts. She was happy her family wanted to see Tony, but she finally said, "If you want to know why Tony isn't here, or tell him how much you miss him, you need to call him directly. I'm not conveying those messages anymore."

The nagging stopped.

Communication

45. What do you mean by communication and why is it so important?

The advice you'll hear most often as you prepare for marriage is this: Be sure to communicate. It sounds more formal than it truly is in practice. Communication simply means the way in which couples convey information to one another and it includes not just talking, but gestures of affection, eye contact, and written notes. It also includes the tone in which thoughts and feelings are communicated. There is no one right way to communicate. The styles will be unique to each couple.

Longtime married couples will tell you, however, that talking with one another on a daily basis is essential. How you touch base will be up to you as a couple, but setting aside a time to talk each day is a good habit to start early in your relationship. Becky and Tony's morning coffee hour together is sacred. If the phone rings during that hour, they don't answer. They read the newspaper, talk about world events, and then tell each other what they have planned for the day.

Couples stay in tune with each other by sharing the details of one another's days. Trading information about the logistics of daily life together is important, whether this is done in person, by phone, or even E-mail. But couples can also get caught in the trap of only talking minutiae with one another and they can sometimes hide by using distancing sorts of communication, such as E-mail. That's why couples should get in the habit of asking each other questions in person, and not just about the day's events. Sometimes asking questions does not come naturally, but it can be learned with practice. Asking questions conveys the message that you are truly interested in your partner's schedule, as well as knowing his or her values, hopes, and dreams.

46. When my fiancé and I fight, we often go days without speaking to one another. Is this a danger sign?

In Psalm 88, a prayer of lament, the psalmist describes how it feels when his friends and neighbors shun him: "You have made me a thing of horror to them. I am shut in so that I cannot escape; …my companions are in darkness" (8, 18). The silent treatment— as not speaking to one another is often called—is an intense form of shunning. When you shun your partner, that person becomes invisible, unworthy, counted out. It's a lonely, terrible place. After a fight, some couples go days and sometimes weeks without speaking to one another, except in very rudimentary and distant ways. The silent treatment can "feel" right after a fight, but it's always a rejection and a closed door. Many couples who split up say later that it was during silent-treatment periods that the seeds of separation were sown in their minds. No matter how angry you are with one another, always use some words of hope. If you need to be by yourself after a fight, explain that you want to be alone for a while but hope you'll be able to talk things over in a calm way later on. Then, take a drive, go visit friends or family, and sort things through.

47. My fiancée says I am not a good listener. I think I am, but why is it so important anyway?

Listening well means not interrupting, giving advice, or presenting solutions. It simply means keeping your own mouth quiet and really paying attention as your loved one speaks. It means asking simple questions for clarification, such as "Tell me more" or "What exactly do you mean?"

Sharon and Al, a St. Thomas More Love Circle couple, had to learn how to adjust to each other's communication styles early in their marriage; it can still sometimes be a challenge. "I like to talk about what I'm going through. And his reaction is to fix it," Sharon says. "I'll say that something at school drove me nuts and he'll say 'just quit.' I don't want to quit. I don't want him to fix it. I just want to talk about it." Sharon says that if you're a fixer type, it's important to just stop and listen.

Wayne Muller, a minister, therapist, and author, once said that the best thing we can do for others in emotional need is this: "Be in their physical presence, with a hand to be held, an open heart, a clear mind, and let grace do the rest." Muller's formula is a good one to keep in mind as you find your unique communication style as a couple.

48. We've heard that marriage is more than a 50-50 proposition. What is meant by that? Shouldn't both give 100 percent?

Marriage isn't a 50-50 proposition because both people should be there 100 percent for the other. But almost always one person in the couple will have more needs than the other, if only for a few hours or a few days. Making the leap of faith into marriage requires that you be open to this imbalance of needs. Both people need to give in a relationship, and in certain areas of marriage, such as the sharing of household duties, you can try to distribute things 50-50. But if one partner consistently does more to keep the relationship going, then this is an indication of deeper problems. It's best to go into marriage knowing that "for better or for worse" means that sometimes you'll be doing the heavy lifting in the relationship and at other times, your partner will. That's both the reality, and the grace, of marriage.

49. I want to keep my own name. My future husband is against it. We are arguing a lot about this now during our marriage preparation time. How can we resolve this?

In the 1970s, during the height of the women's liberation movement, women began retaining their own last names when they married. It was a way to keep their own identities. Becky kept her last name, as did most of her friends, especially those who married after establishing themselves in professions. Some baby-boomer couples hyphenated their names to indicate the partnership between them. Both practices were novel at the time. Now, some women keep their names and others don't. Or some women use their maiden names professionally and their married names for everything else.

The name choice should primarily be a woman's decision. She is the one, after all, who is expected to give up her name. But couples should discuss this together, and if the issue can't be resolved easily, it usually means something deeper is going on in the relationship, perhaps around the distribution of power between the couple. Pay attention, because the name debate might bring forth important issues you should be attending to during your marriage preparation time.

THREE

HOW DO WE PLAN
THE WEDDING CEREMONY?

When and Where?

50. Why can't Catholics marry on Sundays?

There is no church law which forbids weddings on Sundays. The practice in the United States and other countries is to urge people to hold the ceremony on another day so as not to detract from Mass on Sunday.

51. Is it true you can't get married during Lent?

A person can marry on any day of the year. That does not mean that the local church will always allow a big ceremony. Sensitivity to the congregation needs to be kept in mind. For instance, marrying on Holy Thursday, Good Friday, or Holy Saturday would certainly detract from the church's observance of Jesus' last meal with his friends, as well as his passion and death. Likewise, in the previous days of Lent, where the mood is one of penance and reflection, sensibility to the community usually causes people to mute their celebrations somewhat.

52. What documentation will the church require from my intended spouse and me?

This question is one which frequently confuses people. Thus it might be best to list here the normal paperwork involved:

(1) *A baptismal certificate* for each person *which has been issued within the previous six months.* The church does not want the original document which your family has kept all these years. That means you will need to write the parish where you were baptized and have a new one sent. Sometimes, however, not even an old certificate can be obtained. For instance, a person baptized in another country might not even have an original. Then you might

be asked to suggest someone (for instance, a parent) who can testify that you were baptized.

(2) *Self-testimony forms* which are filled out by the priest/deacon, or some other authorized person connected with the church. Each of you will be asked separately a list of questions. The point of this questionnaire is to establish your freedom to marry in the church. The questions are along these lines: Have you been married before? Are you related to your intended spouse by blood or by marriage? Have you been confirmed and made your first communion? What do your parents think about this marriage (if you are under the age of 18)? Are you being forced into this marriage?

(3) *Witness forms* which will also be filled out by someone else. You will be asked to name one or two witnesses who can and will testify to your freedom to marry. The priest/deacon or coordinator will interview the witnesses and then fill out these forms.

In case your spouse is not a Catholic, there are other forms which the priest/deacon will complete.

53. My future spouse and I met at college. Most of the people who will be present at our wedding are classmates. Must we marry in the bride's or groom's parish, or can we pick another parish?

This situation is an increasing phenomenon in the United States. Society is very mobile. Not only do children relocate, but so do their parents. You may marry in your current parish (whether it be that of the bride or the groom) which might not be your parents' parish. You should be a member of that parish, however, so you should register in that parish well in advance of your wedding. Some parishes require that people wanting to use the church for a wedding be a member for a certain length of time, such as six to nine months. Thus you should not postpone registering in that parish. Sometimes universities, colleges, and high schools have chapels which are not parishes but in which they allow their graduates to be married. Each case is different, so you need to check on this well in advance should you wish to be married in a church which is not a parish church. Some parishes allow people who are not members to use the church. You need to inquire in advance if this is what you are contemplating.

Who's Officiating?

54. What is the role of the priest at the ceremony?

The couple administers the sacrament of marriage to each other. The role of the priest or deacon is that of the official witness of the church. Sometimes circumstances are such that a priest or deacon cannot be present at the ceremony, but that rarely happens.

The priest's role, however, should be seen in a larger context than just official witness. Couples should pick a priest they have a relationship with, if possible. This allows the priest to be able to speak from his heart about the couple and to add to the ceremony some touches that enrich the ritual. Father Dan, for instance, spoke in Italian at one point in the service, in honor of Becky's large Italian family. Also, the priest's role can sometimes last well beyond the wedding ceremony, providing another source of support for a couple. Father Dan has married about thirty couples and keeps in touch with many of them. Those who have been in trouble have contacted him for advice and for listening. He was there at the beginning of their lives together and this provided both a special bond and unique perspective.

55. Must the pastor or associate pastor perform the wedding ceremony, or can we ask a priest or deacon friend to preside?

Sometimes pastors have the policy that only the pastor or his associate (or deacon who serves in the parish) can preside. It is always wise to ask well in advance in your planning. Father Dan, as a Jesuit, has witnessed many marriages yet has never been a parish priest. So he always is a guest of the church where the wedding is performed. He has found that most pastors are very happy that a friend of the bride or groom can preside.

56. My fiancé is Jewish. Can a rabbi perform our ceremony? Can I have a priest present?

The way this question is phrased, it is unclear whether you want both the priest and the rabbi to perform the ceremony. Both can be present on the altar. Only one is the official presider. Ordinarily if the wedding is in the Catholic Church the priest would be the logical person to do this. If you want the rabbi to preside, then you must seek a dispensation from the diocese for this, or seek to hold the wedding in a synagogue. It should be pointed out that not all rabbis or priests are willing to take part in such a ceremony.

57. Since my intended spouse has been married before, can we get married in the church? What plans should we make?

There is no quick answer to this. If a person has been previously married and wishes to marry in the church, that previous marriage must be declared invalid or annulled. If the previous spouse has died, there is no problem marrying again in the church. Frequently enough these issues can be handled very quickly, for example when the previous marriage was declared invalid because the Catholic party was not married in the church. The other possibility is that a person needs to go through the annulment process—which could take many months. In any case you should not set any date for a church wedding until you have found out how the church looks at the previous marriage. To do this you should consult a priest or deacon. They can consult a canon lawyer if necessary and give you a quick answer with regard to the church's view of the status of the previous marriage.

58. Would the church permit me to marry in my fiancé's non-Catholic but Christian church?

Since the end of Vatican II in 1965, the church has increasingly allowed Catholics to marry in the church of their non-Catholic spouse. The couple needs to go through all the preparation which they would do when marrying in a Catholic Church. The priest or deacon who is handling the paperwork needs to ask the bishop for a "Dispensation from Form." Ordinarily this is easily granted. Although the minister performs the ceremony, a priest may be present in such a case.

Wedding Parties

59. Must the best man and the maid of honor be Catholics?

No, that is not a requirement, but they must be adults (at least sixteen years old). Not requiring the witnesses to be Catholic is a big change from the past. Sharon, who belongs to the St. Thomas More Parish Love Circle, said that her mother wasn't allowed to have her own bridesmaids because none of her friends were Catholic. So her husband's sister served as matron of honor. Almost every Catholic who married before 1965 will have a similar story about how their plans were altered to meet church requirements. And meeting the requirements meant excluding a lot of people from participating. These pre-Vatican II rules damaged many relationships between Catholics and the institutional church and some people bear scars to this day.

Modern practice encourages participation by Catholics and non-Catholics and in this outreach to all, the church conveys the message that the couple is sharing this commitment with their entire community, both Catholics and people of differing faith traditions. In recent years, priests presiding at marriages have made it a point to welcome non-Catholics and explain some of what will unfold during the marriage Mass. Some couples also print out guides with the names of the wedding participants and some of the steps involved in the Mass. This gesture also helps non-Catholics feel welcomed.

60. Is there a limit to the number of bridesmaids and grooms-men we can have at our wedding?

Theoretically speaking, there is no limit. From a practical perspective, however, the size and configuration of the church or chapel are among the considerations for making a judgment. Most churches impose a limit. Too many people in the wedding party can turn attention away from the bride and groom as well as from the religious aspect of the ceremony.

61. My future spouse has been married before and has children. Can they be part of the ceremony, such as being best man or maid of honor?

There is no problem with children being included in the ceremony. Certainly sons and daughters who are in their teens can be the best man or the maid of honor if they are sixteen or older. Ben, Tony's then teenaged son, served as his best man.

Vows and Symbols

62. I want to get married in my friend's beautiful apple orchard but was told I can't. Why can't Catholics marry in the outdoors?

You may not know it but you are asking about the difference between a civil and a religious wedding. A civil wedding is a contract between two persons. A religious wedding is a covenant involving God and the community. Unless there is a very good reason to the contrary, the church believes that not only the community but the symbols of religious belief should be part of the ambience of the wedding. A garden wedding, or outdoor setting, does not provide that.

63. How much freedom do we have in planning the ceremony?

Much depends on what type of ceremony you would like to have. Some of the variables are having a Mass versus not having a Mass, the possibility of different readings, the type and amount of music, and so forth. Many parishes have wedding coordinators to help each couple personalize their ceremony. Usually each parish has policies based on experience. These policies might include the possible times of the wedding, the length of the ceremony, the number of people in the wedding party, and the like. Each church is different, but the couple is encouraged to plan the ceremony as much as possible.

64. Must we have a Mass? Many non-Catholics will be present at the wedding and know very little about Catholic ceremonies.

The fact that you have concern for your guests shows a good attitude on your part. No, a Mass is not required, even for two Catholics. Sometimes sensitivity to people who will be present argues against having a Mass. On the other hand, people who attend a Catholic wedding presume that it will be a Catholic Mass and would usually have no difficulty with that.

65. My fiancée's extended family is mostly Protestant. Can they, and the other non-Catholic guests, receive communion at our wedding?

Like the previous question, one can avoid this situation by not having a Mass. If, however, you desire to have a Mass, a difficulty arises if your fiancée is not a Catholic. Should the priest give communion only to you but not to your fiancée? That same difficulty also extends to your fiancée's family. This also puts the priest on the spot since he is authorized to give communion only to Catholics, and, under certain circumstances, to the Christian spouse.[7]

66. Even though my future spouse is not a Catholic, we would like to have a wedding Mass. Is that possible?

Before Vatican II neither a wedding Mass was permitted nor could the "Nuptial Blessing" be given when one of the parties was not a Catholic. Today we realize that a couple needs as much spiritual help as they can obtain. Consequently a wedding Mass is allowed and the Nuptial Blessing can be given even without a Mass. Some of the difficulties which can arise in this situation are discussed in the above two questions.

67. African-American friends of ours recently "jumped the broom" at their Catholic wedding. What is the significance of that custom and can symbols of a couple's ethnic heritage be incorporated into the ceremony?

"Jumping the broom" is a Southern United States custom which has its origin in West Africa. It signifies a "leap" into a new life, which in this case is marriage. This custom combines cultural heritage with a reminder that the couple are committing themselves to each other. It can be incorporated into the marriage ceremony. The broom itself is usually kept as a reminder of the wedding. This and similar ethnic customs are usually easily adapted to the Catholic ceremony. They remind both the marrying couple and the congregation of their ethnic community, from which should come support in their life together.

68. What freedom do my fiancée and I have in writing our own vows and picking the scripture readings?

You may certainly write you own vows. Many couples prefer to do so. The church asks that in the vows you mention that you will be faithful to your partner, and that this is a permanent union. The church also provides a variety of prayers as well as scripture readings for the ceremony. You may choose from these prayers or make up your own. Likewise you may choose from the suggested scripture readings or pick others not listed.

69. We want to read aloud a poem we wrote for one another. Is this allowed?

The simple answer is "yes." It should be in good taste and fit in with the whole ceremony. However, it cannot take the place of the scripture readings.

70. My fiancée and I have a special song, but it doesn't have a spiritual theme. Can it be sung during our wedding ceremony?

Yes, but again it should be in good taste and fit in with the whole ceremony.

71. Do women still have to promise to "obey" their husbands?

It is interesting that you ask this question. The promise of the woman to "obey" her husband is not part of any of the suggested forms of the marriage vows. As pointed out above (cf. question 68), you can write your own marriage vows.

Details and Logistics

72. I want both my parents to walk me down the aisle. Is this allowed?

Not only is it allowed but it is encouraged. In fact the official ritual mentions this as the norm. The custom in the United States has been for the father of the bride to "give her away." That is not a universal custom, however, nor among all Catholic ethnic groups living in the United States.

And if a parent or parents are dead or unavailable, a bride should feel free to choose a person who symbolizes a deep connection to her life. Becky's niece Gretchen asked her two brothers to walk her down the aisle. Their father had died several years before. Gretchen is average size, but her younger brothers are both 6-foot-5 and both closely resemble their deceased father. It was a touching moment of symbolism to see the tall brothers walk their older sister down the aisle. The memory of their father permeated the church and those gathered cried in both sorrow and joy at the scene.

73. What does the wedding ring symbolize? Is it a necessary part of the ceremony?

The wedding ring symbolizes the fidelity which one spouse pledges to the other. In the early part of the twentieth century frequently enough only the groom gave his bride a wedding ring but not vice versa. It is not a necessary part of the ceremony, and in some countries rings are not exchanged.

74. Can we have a unity candle at our ceremony?

The unity candle is a relatively new addition to the wedding ceremony. It symbolizes the oneness of the two families that are united through the marriage of the bride and groom. Although it is not part of the official rite, most couples today like it to be part of the ceremony. This is in line with the freedom of the couple to plan their ceremony.

75. Can we decorate the church with flowers, pictures, and other things?

This is up to the administrators of the church or chapel where the wedding takes place. Usually each parish has a policy on this. People can easily forget that on a given day other activities take place at the church—and that their wedding is not the only event. This has to be kept in mind when asking about decorating. And couples can get creative here. Tony and Becky attended a wedding in a rural church that was near a lake where the bride spent her summers as a child. Instead of bouquets, the bride and attendants carried stylized bouquets of wheat. They provided a symbol of the rural countryside surrounding the lake, as well as a beautiful and unique decoration that didn't require altering the interior of the small country church in any way.

76. Can we throw rice at the end of the service?

Each church usually has a policy on this. One question that always needs to be answered is "who will clean up the rice in a timely manner?" If the parish does not have a janitor, or if the wedding takes place on a day when the janitor is not working, someone needs to take care of this practical problem.

In recent years, couples have gotten creative in the rice department. Some give their guests birdseed to throw, or small balloons to release as the couple exits the church. At one couple's wedding, each guest was handed a small vial of bubbles and instructed to blow them at the bride and groom as they walked down the stairs of the church. It was beautiful and left no mess to clean up.

77. How much are we supposed to pay the people involved in our ceremony, including the priest, the musicians, and the parish wedding coordinator?

Usually parishes or chapels have set fees for renting the church. These fees may or may not include the musicians or the parish wedding coordinator. A gift to the priest or deacon is not ordinarily included. What some do is to look at the entire cost of the wedding and reception and give the church a percentage of the total. When people look at it that way, they usually find out that they give very little to the church when compared to the other costs. Yet the church is where the attention is focused.

78. Is it okay to take photographs and videotape the ceremony?

Ordinarily pictures are taken of the church and the wedding party before and/or after the ceremony. Although nothing intrinsically is wrong with taking photos during the ceremony itself or videotaping everything, some churches ban doing so because of the way they can sometimes be intrusive on the ceremony. Other churches do not mind, as long as the flash is minimized and the videotaping is done quietly and unobtrusively.

79. Are there any state regulations we should be aware of?

Each state has its own set of laws governing the celebration of marriage. Such laws concern the timeliness in obtaining the wedding license, authorizing who can perform the ceremony, the number of witnesses, and so on. What is true in one state may not be true in another. It is always good to check with the church *where the wedding will take place* to see what state laws are applicable.

Four

After the Marriage Ceremony

The First-Year Challenge

80. Older married couples have told us that there can be a letdown after the wedding and the honeymoon. Why is that? How can we prevent that letdown?

One young woman planned a storybook wedding—beautiful gowns, exquisite decorations. The reception was perfect too—plenty of wine, great food, dancing, and a masterful slide show that showed the bride and groom as babies, teens, young people, and finally showed them together as the lovely couple. After the wedding and the honeymoon, the couple returned home to their new home and to their jobs. The bride felt a complete letdown. She had always fantasized about the wedding, but not the marriage. When reality set in, she felt let down. She worked through it after several months, but she can still remember, a decade later, how disillusioned she felt about the reality of marriage.

In our culture, we have very few guideposts showing us how to navigate the everydayness of marriage. Romantic movies usually end with the couple walking down the aisle or planning the trip down the aisle. And often in the months leading up to the marriage, everyone is so busy and excited, it's impossible for reality to sink in.

So when it finally does, it can be a shocker. Think of going back to work on a Monday morning after a perfect vacation. That's the letdown feeling some couples describe as they tackle the nitty-gritty of married life—jobs, in-laws, money woes.

Sharon and Al, a Love Circle couple, dated in college. After they married, they moved to a small town where Al's family lived. Sharon remembers: "It was his territory. I didn't know anybody there. I was in a little apartment that took me about ten minutes to clean. I didn't know a soul. We didn't have any money. On the weekends, we'd go visit his folks. He was out doing farm work with his dad and I was in the kitchen with his mom. This wasn't how I envisioned marriage. There was a letdown for me. You can't prevent it necessarily. You just have to learn to communicate and work through it."

81. Longtime married couples say that, looking back, their first year of marriage was one of the hardest years. Why is that so?

The first year of marriage can be difficult because everything is so new and couples are still in the getting-to-know-one-another stage, even if the couples lived together before marriage. James Hillman, in his book *The Soul's Code,* says when people sink roots they are "growing down." The challenge the first year of marriage is to sink roots to nourish a strong, secure base from which the marriage can grow.

As courtship, romance, and engagement excitement wear off, couples are left with life's more mundane concerns: How do we spend our money? Where do we spend holidays? Who pays the bills? Couples learn how to negotiate the time they spend together and spend apart. It's in the first year, too, that family-of-origin differences surface.

Sherry and Steve, a Love Circle couple, grew up in dramatically different households. She was Lutheran. He was Catholic. He is Italian and his extended family seemed huge and loud to Sherry, an only child. She felt culture shock that first year of marriage. "I was not used to the loudness, the hands-on, the touchy-feely," Sherry remembers. "I love it now, but it took some getting used to. Even financially, his parents were better off than mine."

82. Longtime married couples say most of their fights the first year centered on the distribution of household chores, such as who does the laundry, cooking, yard work. This seems so mundane. What is going on?

Pay close attention to your arguments about household chores during your first year of marriage. Though mundane on the surface, household-duty fights almost always stem from deeper issues. They can help expose, early on, the fault lines of the marriage. This will allow you to tackle such problems early before those fault lines crack open and threaten the life of your relationship.

Couples project onto household duties many issues unresolved from childhood. For instance, two women who were friends married men who were raised in alcoholic homes. Both men, fleeing from the chaos they remembered as children, grew agitated when the rooms in their adult homes got cluttered. Both of their wives, in the first year of marriage, felt uncomfortable with the husbands' agitation and rather than insist that the husbands uncover the root cause of their agitation, the women spent too much of their time cleaning their homes to keep their husbands happy. After a few years, and after children came along, both wives grew more and more resentful at all the housework and insisted that their husbands do more to help keep the homes clean. The husbands took this as relentless nagging and did very little to remedy the situation, which made both wives even angrier. It took major crises in both marriages to crack open the root cause of the clean-home syndrome and the destructive dynamic it started in both of these marriages.

Couples need to divide household chores that first year of marriage along lines of ability and preference, being careful not to assign duties based on gender lines (women do the dishes; men mow the lawn) unless those are the duties each wishes to pursue. Also, care should be taken not to assign chores based on the chores your mothers and fathers did in the homes you grew up in. This can set up unreasonable expectations and comparisons. As a couple you need to be willing to renegotiate duties as your life circumstances change, especially when moving from house to apartment—and after the children come along.

Sharon, a Love Circle member, did all the cooking, and the cleaning, and the wash when she and Al married thirty years ago. He did the outdoor stuff—the lawn and the car. Later, when there were more things going on, Sharon's resentment grew at how much of the work she was shouldering. "I finally learned that I had to tell him if I needed some help, instead of standing in the kitchen wondering why he wasn't in there helping me. Couples should let each other know if they feel overwhelmed and need some help. And they should find out what each other likes to do. I wouldn't want to do the cars. I like to do the checkbook and he doesn't. You should each focus on your strengths."

If both of you work, and time is more of an issue than money is, discuss whether hiring a housekeeper would free up more time and energy for each of you. It can be a wise investment for a marriage. And finally, pay attention when you have repeated arguments over one specific household task. It could be a clue to deeper issues in your marriage that need attention.

83. Longtime married couples also say that fighting (and not just about housework) is part of all healthy marriages. But how can we learn to do healthy fighting our first year of marriage?

John Gottman, a University of Washington professor and author of several books on marriage, including the excellent *Seven Principles for Making Marriage Work,* can accurately predict a couple's chances of divorcing, sometimes within five minutes of meeting them. He watches couples argue, and from their arguing styles can predict—with 91 percent accuracy—which couples will divorce within four years.

Pay attention to your fighting style the first year of marriage. If you use a lot of sarcasm, cynicism, name-calling, and mockery, these are all red flags. And if there is any physical abuse of any kind, the marriage needs intervention right away. People who have left abusive marriages say that the physical violence often began the first year, but was glossed over and forgotten once the couple made up. But physical violence in a marriage almost always increases, unless the couple seeks help right away.

Healthy fighting is marked by using "I" statements about feelings and thoughts. Accusative "You always" statements build defenses rather than true communication. Healthy fighting will differ from couple to couple. Some couples never go to bed angry. Other couples set timers and give one another five minutes to vent. Some do post-mortems after the fights end and tell each other honestly how certain fighting styles do much more damage than good.

In the first years of their marriage, Becky would often say, in the middle of a heated argument, "Well, maybe I just need to move out for a while." Having been raised in a dramatic family where hyperbole was often the only way to get an important point across, Becky didn't mean it about moving out. But Tony was raised in a family where people used words sparingly and honestly, so that when she said she was thinking of moving out, he believed her.

Arguing loudly and passionately can actually be good for a marriage. It can clear the air and couples often speak the truth during intense arguments, and this truth can break up emotional log-jams in the marriage. As long as you aren't hitting one another or using excessive sarcasm and verbal cruelty, there is no one correct way to argue. But it is important to watch the fighting habits that develop the first year. These tend to stick.

84. Why is it so hard to find time for each other during the first year of marriage?

Dating is a natural part of courtship. Couples set aside time to focus on themselves as a couple. When couples marry, they often forget to schedule in the couple time because they are together at home. But when you are at home, it's easy—and often necessary—to do your own chores, work, hobbies. Parallel play happens when children play with their own toys but in each other's company. They play side by side, or in the same room, without much interaction. It's a natural evolutionary step in child development.

"Parallel work and play" for married couples happens when you're both in the house, but doing your own things, often in separate areas of your home. This is a natural step for a couple to take. No one can be with another person every moment. But in the first year of marriage, couples sometimes do too much parallel play and work and not enough interacting.

Couple rhythms change after marriage. The stress of the wedding is over. Sometimes couples have moved to new towns and begun new jobs, or they've moved into a new home and face a long list of settling-in chores.

There are ways to make more time to spend together. Dating is important (see the answer to question 95), and also setting aside special times each week in the home to be in one another's company. For some, it's Sunday mornings in bed with coffee and the newspaper. For others, it's Friday night at home cooking a nice meal and watching a movie together. It doesn't matter what the practice is, what matters is setting aside some special time in your home to just be with one another.

85. What problems arise in the first year of marriage concerning expectations of your spouse?

One of the biggies is expecting that your partner will know what you need from him or her, and then feeling disappointed or angry when the partner fails to deliver what you expected. This problem can be avoided by one simple rule: Ask for what you need. Couples often don't ask each other for what they need because they fear being rejected. Or they feel they don't have a right to ask for anything. Your partner might say no to your request, but at least the request is out in the open for discussion. This is an important habit to establish early in the marriage. Remind each other that you aren't mind readers. If you need something, ask. And ask in the most direct language possible. Practice "owning your needs" in the first year of marriage and you'll avoid much grief later on.

86. What financial decisions must be made the first year of marriage?

If you sit down and ask and answer these basic questions right at the beginning, you should have most of the major money decisions handled:

1. Will we have joint bank accounts, retain separate accounts, or have a combination of both?
2. Who will be in charge of actually sitting down and writing out the checks (or paying the bills on the Internet)?
3. Will we make out a budget?
4. How much credit card debt are we comfortable having?
5. How will debts be paid off? (This includes student loans.)
6. How much of our income should we save?
7. What longer-term financial goals (buying a home, saving for a baby) do we have as a couple?
8. What is our plan to save that money?
9. What are our greatest fears about money?
10. Do we need to get help from a professional financial planner to work out our finances as a couple?

87. Does a person start to lose his or her individual personality or self-image in that first year of marriage?

A couple named Molly and Jeff are alike in many ways. They are smart, ambitious, athletic, and have similar families and educational backgrounds. They are both quiet, but have terrific senses of humor. People say about them, "Oh no wonder Molly and Jeff got together, they are so much alike."

The priest who did their marriage preparation with them gave them one key piece of advice. He told them that while marriage is very much a union, they should remember to look for the "other" in the spouse. If you forget the otherness of the spouse, and the otherness of yourself, he said, you risk identifying too strongly with your coupleness. When this happens, someone's needs, desires, and dreams will inevitably get ignored, setting up problems for the future. One young woman put her husband through law school; it had been her goal as well. She then raised the children at home and one day, at midlife, woke up and realized that her *own* dreams and ambitions had been lost along the way. She was fifty years old and had no idea who she really was. She moved out for three months and did a lot of soul searching, trying to remember who she was at nineteen, when she married her husband. She revived some interests she had let go of early on, renewed some old friendships, and made a list of goals that were hers alone for personal growth. After some counseling, she moved back home.

Marriages grow stronger when the wife and the husband each retain their own interests and dreams, in addition to dreams they hold together. To retain this "otherness," it's important to spend time by yourself, nurture friendships, pursue hobbies, take classes, and on occasion visit your parents and family without your spouse. Remember the person you were before marriage. That person is still there and needs some attention.

88. What kind of stance toward outside relationships does a newly married couple need to adopt?

Your most important relationship—and your first loyalty— is to your marriage. All other relationships should be evaluated in the ways they hurt, or help, your marriage. An important decision to make as a couple in your first year of marriage is how you will handle contact with former boyfriends and girlfriends. The Internet has made it quite easy to stay in touch with people living all over the world. Margaret and Ken follow this intelligent rule: If contacted by a former love interest, they always tell each other. This way it's out in the open and removes the "secret" nature from the contact. Couples can then decide together whether the contact is healthy and okay for the marriage, or whether it has the potential to cause problems.

Outside relationships include work relationships with members of the opposite sex. If you are socializing a lot (lunches, coffee, after-work drinks) with a coworker of the opposite sex and keeping that fact from your spouse, this is a red flag.

In the Internet age, it is especially important to be open about outside relationships because women and men can develop emotional relationships with strangers they meet online. Online relationships should never be kept secret, because they have great potential to drive couples apart. The most important relationship is the marriage itself. Keep this in mind, and the solutions to outside relationships will be easier.

89. How do relationships with friends change?

Couples sometimes make the mistake of letting go of old friends that first year of marriage, especially if the friends are not married. But women and men draw a lot of support from their same-sex friends. Girls' Night Out and Boys' Night Out can be fun and also provide a break for couples from one another's company. Remember, don't expect your spouse to provide all your fun; it's too much pressure and places an unrealistic expectation on your partner.

A note of caution: If your spouse discourages you from seeing your friends and puts them down as a way to turn you against them, this could be the beginning of an abusive relationship. Most abusive relationships begin with the tearing down of friends, and then a partner's insistence that you isolate yourself from those friends. It's a way of controlling the other person and often escalates into physical violence. If this behavior begins in your first year of marriage pay attention, talk about it, and seek professional help.

90. How can the first year of marriage be joyful rather than just a series of adjustments and misunderstandings?

A young woman who is a broadcast journalism executive in Boston has met famous people and traveled the world. She said recently that the only thing she is in awe of anymore is "a good time." The first year can be difficult as couples negotiate together the path they will walk upon the rest of their marriage. It can be intense, especially if money is tight, as it sometimes is for couples who marry young.

One antidote? Remember to have some fun; schedule it in. Take an evening to recount the joys in your life since you married. Play the "Five Best Things about Being Married" game: list the five best things about your marriage that bring you happiness and joy. The game sounds corny, and you might feel silly while making your lists, but it actually will help you remember the reasons you came together in the first place and what keeps you together. If you find there's not a lot of joy in your marriage, then it's a signal to actively seek it and to nurture it when you find it. First Thessalonians reminds us to "rejoice always." A tall order, but a great ideal.

91. What resources are available for us in the Catholic Church to guide us through the first year of marriage?

Ideally, each parish should offer some support for newly married couples. At St. Aloysius parish in Spokane, the weekday Mass on the first Tuesday of the month is offered for newly married couples. It seems like a small thing, but it sends the message that the newlyweds in the faith community are in the thoughts and prayers of the entire church.

Ask about and seek out programs and workshops at your parish or in the diocese. If no mentor program with older couples exists in your parish, offer to help start a program. Usually *Marriage Encounter* is geared toward longer-married couples, but ask around your diocese, or get in touch with the people who led your *Engaged Encounter,* to see what resources are available. Going on retreat together is another option.

The Catholic Church you attend might also offer services for more serious problems in marriage. Some dioceses sponsor safe shelters and other types of support for battered spouses. And counseling is often available through Catholic Charities.

Faith Sharing

92. How important is it to join a faith community right away?

It is important in the first year to establish what church you'll attend. It should be a mutual decision. This is especially important if you belong to different faith traditions. Julie and Grant, a Love Circle couple, were married in a Lutheran church. "Grant was a strong Catholic and I thought we'd go to the Lutheran Church once in awhile. Well, we went to the Catholic Church that first Sunday. The second Sunday was the same and the third Sunday was the same. Pretty soon I said maybe we should go to the Lutheran Church and he said, 'No honey, I'm a Catholic and I can't do it.' This should have been resolved before our marriage."

Eventually Julie became a Catholic, but she and Grant urge other couples to discuss their choice of church before their wedding, since the church is such a strong source of support for a newly married couple.

After Steve and Sherry married thirty-two years ago, this Love Circle couple realized that they had less in common with their single friends than before. Steve has also realized that in workplaces, where many people spend the bulk of their days, it can be hard to find support for strong marriages. Often, at work, someone is going through a divorce or is down on marriage.

Steve and Sherry drew strength from the fact their marriage was a sacrament. They found others who felt the same. "If you are with people who believe in marriage, especially the sacrament of marriage, it's a tremendous help," Steve said.

Joining a faith community also provides some built-in marriage mentors. You'll have a chance to meet couples at various stages of their marriages and you can seek them out for advice. A faith community also offers volunteer and service opportunities that couples can do together, such as teaching Sunday school or helping to build a Habitat-for-Humanity home. If you are new in the area, your church can also help connect you with couples your own age, which is important to feeling part of a faith community.

93. Do we need to attend church together?

All the Love Circle couples attend church together because, as Sharon said, "Marriage is a three-way proposition—between a husband, a wife, and God. The more you have that faith in God in your life, the stronger your marriage. And it can get you through those times when you aren't strong."

The couples like the feeling of being with one another and experiencing spirituality together. Liturgy offers opportunities to grow as a couple. After church, couples can talk about the readings or the homily and these conversations might lead them into topics they don't ordinarily discuss. Embraces during the Kiss of Peace can provide an opportunity to forgive a misunderstanding. Spending an hour each week in sacred space with one another is just an opportunity to remember the sacredness of the sacrament that is marriage.

Traditions

94. We received hundreds of wedding presents. Who should write the thank-you notes?

Both of you! Writing thank-you notes can seem a tedious task, but it might help to see it as a spiritual experience you can share. It can be an enriching experience of gratitude for a newly married couple. Sherry and Steve realized that most of the presents were given to them by older couples in the church. Sherry said, "They were looking at us as a couple in the church. The thank-you notes were a spiritual tie to them, a bond."

Writing thank-you notes together might establish, early in your marriage, the recognition that chores should not be divided along gender lines. In many marriages, the woman is unofficially assigned the role of organizing the social life of the couple and this includes accepting or declining invitations and writing thank-you notes. Assigning all social obligation duties to one partner only can build resentment down the road.

95. Are there any traditions which we should set up right away as a couple that will help keep our marriage strong?

Traditions in a marriage help remind a husband and wife of their "coupleness." Traditions also rekindle romance. One tradition many long-time married couples recommend is going out on regular dates—to dinner, or to a concert, or making time for an activity that was enjoyed together while courting. Placing weekly or monthly "dates" with one another on the calendar might seem ridiculous (you are married now and can do stuff together all the time), but "dating" is a good way for couples to remember why they enjoyed being together in the first place. Establishing the tradition in the first year of marriage is important, because it then has a chance of turning into a habit, one that will continue even after their lives grow busy with children.

When they married thirty-two years ago, Jack and Rosalie, another Love Circle couple, didn't go on a honeymoon because of Jack's military commitments. "So we established right away that every year on our anniversary we would go somewhere," Rosalie said. "We still do that now, every year. We take a day off. There were some years we were so poor we couldn't buy two movie tickets, but we'd get rid of the kids—my sister or friend would take them—and we'd go to the park with a picnic, or something. But we'd always celebrate our anniversary."

It's important to get out of the house to have those dates, too, because the temptation at home is to do household chores. Even if you simply take a long walk together, it's a reminder that you wanted to be together because you enjoyed one another's company.

96. We are both part of big, extended families. This first Thanksgiving and Christmas everyone wants us at *their* house. How do we decide where to spend the holidays?

If you recall, family relationships was one area covered in marriage preparation—and here's why. When you marry, your spouse becomes the first person in your newly created family of origin. Your spouse needs to become the No. 1 priority in your life. Holiday decisions sometimes present the first big opportunity to make this clear to the rest of your family.

If you establish this in your first year of marriage, it will become easier in the years ahead. Before the holidays come, sit down together as a couple and decide what you really would like to do. This puts you in control, so that when the invitations come, you can say, "We have decided this year to...." You might want to celebrate the holidays alone. Or go to Thanksgiving at one family's house and Christmas at the other family's house. And then switch holidays the next year. Or you might want to do something a little different each year.

Julie and Grant spent their first Christmas alone because they had just moved to California and no family lived nearby. It remains, thirty-four years later, one of their fondest memories: "It was really special. We had our Christmas tree. We did it the way we wanted. It made us very close," Julie remembers.

Remember to be fair to each other about spending time with both families, if this is something you desire.

Becky's niece, Nichole, recently announced that this year she and her husband and their two young boys will go out of town together for Thanksgiving. They hosted Thanksgiving at their house last year and it was exhausting. They learned that holiday stress can be wearing to a marriage. When children come along, the stress of visiting family every holiday can be overwhelming. Rosalie remembers putting her kids in the car one Christmas Day to visit relatives. All three children cried. "They didn't want to leave home. I thought, 'I'm not going to put them through this.'" She remembered the scene when her own daughter married and moved away from Spokane to San Jose. Rosalie and Jack really wanted to be with her on Christmas, but they said to the young couple, "You do what you want to do. We will never impose on you." Now Rosalie and Jack are delighted to be invited down to San Jose.

The Love Circle couples warn newly married couples that the holiday challenge might be the biggest one of their first year. Their advice: Make your decision and stick to it. "It should be between the two of them and they shouldn't cave under pressure," Sherry said. "They might need to write letters to both sides of the family."

Making a decision about holidays is good practice for later marriage pressures from families, such as who can be in the labor room during the birth of a child, and so forth. Make your decision and then hold your ground.

Final Thoughts

97. One older couple told us to remember to treat each other the kind way we treat strangers and acquaintances. What exactly do they mean?

Couples often forget to extend some simple courtesies to one another that they extend to strangers and acquaintances. This means saying please and remembering to say thank you. Marriage can sometimes be an excuse to forget manners and thoughtfulness. These might seem like unimportant gestures, but kindness conveys care and attention. Before Becky married Tony she traveled a lot with newspaper colleagues. She was fascinated when one wife met her husband at the airport wearing dirty sweatpants. She complained to her husband right away about some problems at home. She didn't ask, "How was your flight?" and she didn't offer any of the common courtesies she might have extended to a friend or acquaintance after a long flight. Becky vowed that if she ever married, she'd always dress up and be cheerful when greeting her husband upon his return from a trip. She has kept that vow.

98. Do couples generally set new goals after they marry?

They should. It's important to sit down and talk about some short-term and long-term goals. Setting goals is an important marriage exercise. It can "seal" your coupleness, because it forces you to look toward the future as a unit, as a family. Couples who ultimately split sometimes say they grew in different directions. Setting goals together, and sitting down on a regular basis to see how you're meeting those goals, is one way to prevent growing apart.

99. Can Catholics divorce?

Catholics have divorced since the beginning of the church. Sometimes this has been an informal departure of one of the spouses; in other cases it has involved a legal process. In the

United States the courts act as a neutral third party in protecting the children and in dividing the assets. Divorce should be the last resort, and only be sought when all other reasonable solutions have failed to keep the partners living together peaceably. From a theological viewpoint, the problem is not divorce, but remarriage after divorce.

100. What is the role of the annulment process?

Catholics do sometimes remarry after divorce. For many years they were not allowed to do so in the church, except in rare circumstances and under certain conditions. Over the last half century the church has changed her attitude on this issue. Instead of viewing marriage as a contract, since Vatican II the church looks at it as a covenant, a lifetime intimate partnership of life and love (cf. question 9). In an annulment process, the church looks at the evidence to see if that intimate partnership (in other words, a truly sacramental marriage) existed. If the church decides that a sacramental marriage never existed, then she grants an annulment which allows the parties to remarry in the church. We can understand this better if we look at divorce among family members and friends. A divorce usually indicates that something has kept the marriage from being a lasting union. The causes of a divorce usually have been present for some time before the actual separation takes place. Likewise, when the church judges an annulment petition, the church looks at the causes of the separation and then makes a judgment as to whether a true sacramental marriage ever existed.

101. Finally, is there any overall advice you would give a couple who plan to marry?

Remember that each couple is unique, just as individuals are unique. Advice from other couples, from books, from videos, from workshops, from *Engaged Encounters* will help, but always be mindful and respectful of the relationship that is uniquely yours. You know it the best.

Older couples will tell you about the importance of "working at your marriage." This means paying attention to it. This means nurturing the relationship through shared experiences. This means sitting down and talking through issues large and small. This means having some fun, going on dates. This means owning your own needs, and asking your spouse for what you need from him or her. This means not being too proud or too embarrassed to seek outside help if problems in your marriage seem overwhelming.

Remember that your marriage belongs to you as a couple and no one else. Treasure it, protect it, allow it to grow and mature. And don't forget to pray for your marriage. The "movement of the spirit" through a marriage is a powerful aid, through good times and bad, through rich and poor, through sickness and health.

Good luck! And may God bless your marriage.

NOTES

1. Ludwig Ott, *Fundamentals of Catholic Dogma* (St. Louis: B. Herder, 1952), 460, 462.

2. *The Church Today,* ## 48–50. This particular reference is taken from Walter Abbott and Joseph Gallagher (eds.), *The Documents of Vatican II* (New York: America Press, 1966), 250–55.

3. Jean Carbon, *The Wellspring of Worship* (Eugene, OR: Wipf and Stock, 2001), 117.

4. Amy Vanderbilt, *Everyday Etiquette* (New York: Bantam Books, 1952), 83.

5. David Popenoe and Barbara Dafoe Whitehead. "Should We Live Together?" Executive Summary, *National Marriage Project* (Rutgers University, June 2002). *http://marriage.rutgers.edu/Publications/SWLT2%20TEXT.htm*

6. Joseph F. Eagan, *Restoration and Renewal: The Church in the Third Millennium* (Kansas City: Sheed & Ward, 1995), 346.

7. *Code of Canon Law* (Washington, DC: Canon Law Society of America, 1983), Canon 844, 3.

FOR FURTHER READING

Finley, Kathy. *The Seeker's Guide to Building a Christian Marriage: Eleven Essential Skills*. Chicago: Loyola Press, 2000.

Gottman, John and Nan Silver. *The Seven Principles for Making Marriage Work*. New York: Crown Publications, 1999.

Hayden, Ruth. *For Richer, Not Poorer—The Money Book for Couples*. Deerfield Beach: Health Communications, 1999.

Hite, Shere. *The Hite Report: A National Study of Female Sexuality*. New York: Seven Stories Press, 2003.

———. *The Hite Report on Male Sexuality*. New York: Ballantine Books, 1987.

Peck, M. Scott. *The Road Less Traveled, 25th Anniversary Edition*. New York: Touchstone Books, 2003.

Prather, Hugh and Gayle Prather. *I Will Never Leave You: How Couples Can Achieve the Power of Everlasting Love*. New York: Bantam Books, 1995.

Whitehead, Evelyn Eaton and James D. Whitehead. *Marrying Well: Possibilities in Christian Marriage*. Garden City, NY: Doubleday, 1981.

———. *The Wisdom of the Body: Making Sense of Our Sexuality*. New York: Crossroad, 2001.

*Other Books
in This Series*

101 QUESTIONS AND ANSWERS ON THE BIBLE
by Raymond E. Brown, S.S.

101 QUESTIONS AND ANSWERS ON THE BIBLICAL TORAH
by Roland E. Murphy, O. Carm.

101 QUESTIONS AND ANSWERS ON THE CHURCH
by Richard P. McBrien

101 QUESTIONS AND ANSWERS ON CONFUCIANISM,
DAOISM, AND SHINTO
by John Renard

101 QUESTIONS AND ANSWERS ON DEACONS
by William T. Ditewig

101 QUESTIONS AND ANSWERS ON ISLAM
by John Renard

101 QUESTIONS AND ANSWERS ON PAUL
by Ronald D. Witherup

101 QUESTIONS AND ANSWERS ON VATICAN II
by Maureen Sullivan, O.P.

*Other Books
Under the Former Series Title*

RESPONSES TO 101 QUESTIONS ON THE DEAD SEA SCROLLS
by Joseph A. Fitzmyer, S.J.

RESPONSES TO 101 QUESTIONS ABOUT JESUS
by Michael L. Cook, S.J.

RESPONSES TO 101 QUESTIONS ABOUT FEMINISM
by Denise Lardner Carmody

RESPONSES TO 101 QUESTIONS ON THE PSALMS
AND OTHER WRITINGS
by Roland E. Murphy, O. Carm.

RESPONSES TO 101 QUESTIONS ON DEATH AND
ETERNAL LIFE
by Peter C. Phan

RESPONSES TO 101 QUESTIONS ON HINDUISM
by John Renard

RESPONSES TO 101 QUESTIONS ON BUDDHISM
by John Renard

RESPONSES TO 101 QUESTIONS ON THE MASS
by Kevin W. Irwin

RESPONSES TO 101 QUESTIONS ON GOD AND EVOLUTION
by John F. Haught

RESPONSES TO 101 QUESTIONS ON
CATHOLIC SOCIAL TEACHING
by Kenneth R. Himes, O.F.M.